MASTERPIECES OF INDIAN SCULPTURE

MASTERPIECES OF

NDIAN SCULPTURE

C. SIVARAMAMURTI

NATIONAL MUSEUM, NEW DELHI

National Museum
First edition: 1971
Second edition: 1996

Price: Rs. 90/-

Layout and design : Kushal Pal

Production : Sanjib Kumar Singh

Sole Distributors : The Publications Division, Patiala House, New Delhi

Published by : Dr R.R.S. Chauhan for National Museum, Janpath, New Delhi
Printed by : Creative Offset, Delhi-95

ISBN No. : 81-85832-05-6

FOREWORD

This album of Masterpieces of Indian Sculpture by late C. Sivaramamurti has been in great demand among the visitors from all walks of life. Since all the copies of its first edition have been sold out, its reprint appeared to be an unavoidable necessity and hence this editon. I am sure that this book will continue to inspire the lovers of Indian art, history and culture as has been the case with all the publications of late C. Sivaramamurti. The efforts made by the enthusiastic team of publication unit of National Museum in redesigning this edition deserve my deep appreciation.

National Museum
New Delhi

Dr. S.S. Biswas
(Director General)

INTRODUCTION

Indian Art is kaleidoscopic in its rich variety of form and colour. Sculpture, for its feeling of depth and modelling, has claimed the first place of importance, and has been styled *chitra*. Carving in relief and painting, as *ardhachitra* and *chitrābhāsa* respectively, come next.

From the earliest historical periods, magnificent sculptures have been fashioned by craftsmen all over the land, and compose the different schools, known geographically and in a vast space of history, covering over two thousand years.

After the wane of the Mauryan power, the Suṅgas and the Sātavāhanas, who ruled in the North and in the Deccan respectively, carried on the traditions of their predecessors. There is no better monument than what remains of the rail, that surrounded the Bharhut *stūpa,* to illustrate the best of Śuṅga art. There are panels on the coping, uprights and crossbars, illustrating important scenes from the life of Buddha and incidents from his previous lives, known as the *Jātakas.* A coping piece (Plate I), recently acquired by the National Museum, is a rare work of art, illustrating the division of the relics of Buddha, which were carried by the royal recipients in reliquaries placed on elephants. The musical scene beside it illustrates the funeral celebrations. A carving, with an exactly similar scene, occurs in Sātavāhana sculpture of the 2nd century A.D., at Amarāvati, also on rail coping.

The Sātavāhanas who ruled in the Deccan were a powerful dynasty of kings whose empire extended from the Western to the Eastern coast. In Western India there were several caves excavated during the rule of the Sātavāhanas. These Buddhist *chaityas* and *vihāras* are famous for their architectual and sculptural elegance. The Sātavāhanas were similarly responsible for carving the exquisite rail, in about the 2nd century A.D., at Amarāvatī, on the banks of the Krishṇā, through the inspiration of Nāgārjuna, the great Buddhist teacher. A few sculptures recovered from Pitalkhora, in an early Western Indian cave, are typical of this phase of early Indian art in the Deccan. A harem scene, representing a prince, accompanied by his royal consort, with attendants all around, is a fine example of Sātavāhana art of the 2nd century B.C. (Plate II). The woollen coverlet for the couch, the elaborate waist zone and heavy anklets as well as the *prabhrashṭaka* flower garland adorning the braid of the princess, the thick waist cord of the prince, *deḍḍubhaka,* as it is known in early literature, are all very intersting.

Almost of the same time is the art of the ivory carvers of Vidiśā who, as the inscription says, fashioned the eastern gateway at Sānchī. It is a fragment from this that the National Museum has recently acquired to illustrate early Sātavāhana art in its galleries. This terminal *toraṇa* architrave (Plate III) illustrates a gay young woman, seated on a rock, with her toilet box and wine pot beside her, in the vicinity of the celestial stream, in which a heavenly elephant is refreshing himself by a dip. The portion illustrating the lover beside her is broken and lost. A seated winged griffin tops the terminal of the architrave.

Of the four sculptures recently received in the National Museum on perpetual loan from the British Museum to represent the art of Amarāvatī, and exquisitely carved image from the rail is a striking example of Sātavāhana art of 150 A.D. (Plate IV). It contains in a medallion and in three panels below a striking narrative sequence of the story of sage Asita's visit. Asita, the hoary sage, arrives at the palace of Śuddhodana to see the new-born Englightened One to be, is announced by the *pratīhārī,* the typical feminine usher, and seated in front of Śuddhodana laments that he would not be alive to listen to the words of wisdom from the child when he would turn the wheel of Law after his englightenment. The carving is delicate, suggestive and full of life and emotion.

Kushāṇa sculpture of the 1st-2nd century A.D. has given the world some of the most lovely examples of feminine charm in art like the Bhutesar *yakshīs.* The National Museum has a unique example of Lakshmī, the Goddess of Prosperity (Plate Va), standing on a brimming vessel, its water suggested by lotuses, pressing her breast, indicating her motherhood and her association with a river goddess, to assure prosperity to the children of the soil through *payas,* viz. water, as a mother would sustain the child by *payas,* viz. milk. The pearly teeth peeping through her mouth indicate joy, as prosperity means joy.

Another example of this period of art from Mathurā is a splendid example of the pleasing theme of mother and child (Plate Vb), the little one being offered a rattle, to receive which it joyfully springs up. A companion of the mother looks on with satisfaction, from behind the screen.

Yet another Kushāṇa example chosen in this series is a corpulent dwarf, Kubera, the Lord of Wealth (Plate VI). His hair arranged as a wig, rotund belly, dreamy eyes and sly smile indicate an indolent, contented attitude of opulence.

The Kushāṇas, who ruled over a great empire that spread beyond the Hindukush and touched Central Asia, had a flourishing school of sculpture in the north-western region, now included in Pakistan, which from the name of the locality has been styled Gāndhāra. It is greatly influenced by Greco-Roman traditions. A fine example of this school illustrates the incident of Nanda following Buddha against his will, with his mind lost in a longing for his beautiful consort Sundarī, whose toilet he had been witnessing a few minutes earlier (Plate VII).

The Ikshvāku rulers, who followed the Sātavāhanas in the Krishṇā valley towards the end of the 2nd century, were responsible for the magnificent monuments at Nāgārjunakoṇḍa and other places, with carvings in a style of the Sātavāhana rulers in this region. One of the finest examples of Ikshvāku art is a casing slab (Plate VIII) from the large *stūpa,* which represents in three tiers of panels, the birth of Buddha, seven steps he walked to assure himself that he would not be born again, but would become the Supremely Enlightened, the casting of the horoscope and the prediction that the new born one would either be a Universal Monarch or the Supremely Enlightened One, the presentation of the child to the family deity, when a miracle occurred, and the visit of Asita, the aged sage, who hurried to have a look at the new born child, as he knew he was nearing his end.

The Guptas, who followed the Kushāṇas in the North, had their powerful contemporaries in the Deccan in the Vākāṭakas, with whom they were matrimonially related. The Gupta phase of art, which is usually styled golden, and which undoubtedly is a great eventful period, has produced some of the greatest masterpieces, including the famous standing Buddha from Mathurā and the preaching Buddha from Sārṇāth. An image of Vishnu (Plate IX) that should take rank with any of the best masterpieces of Gupta art, now in the National Museum, would at once recall the magnificent representation of the deity as Śeshaśāyi at Deogarh.

An exquisite Buddhist carving from Sārnāth of the Gupta period is the inscribed Avalokiteśvara (Plate X a) which is also in the National Museum.

The art of the Vākāṭakas, which has world fame, on account of the magnificent carvings and the paintings at Ajaṇṭā and Ellorā, is here in the National Museum fortunately represented by some bronzes, some of them inscribed in box-headed Brāhmī characters of the period. One of these (Plate X b) is particularly interesting for the flying cherubs, that hover over the master, in the vicinity of an umbrella. These are among the only bronzes of this important phase of art that have yet come to light, and the National Museum is particularly proud of this collection.

Feudatories of the Guptas were Maitrakas who ruled in Gujarat. Some of the early sculptures from Sāmalāji, Roḍā and Iḍār and other places represent the Maitraka phase of art. A recent acquisition in the National Museum is a mother and child from Sāmālaji (Plate XI). The beaming face of the mother and child procalim the sweet age of innocence and the sublimity of motherhood, magnificently depicted by the early Indian sculptor.

From the ceiling of the *maṇdapa* of an early temple from Aihoḷe is a panel (Plate XII) to represent early Western Chāḷukya carving. The Western Chāḷukyas, who succeeded the Vākāṭakas in the 6th century in the Deccan, had created such important temples as the Ladkhan, the Bādāmī caves and a couple of centuries later the richly embellished temples of Paṭṭaḍakal. The movement of the Vidyādharas flying in the air is wonderfully expressed by the opposite direction of the clouds and the fluttering garments as well as by the contour of the body itself on the move.

The Pallavas who ruled in Kāñchīpuram in South India were great devotees of Śiva, and the Somāskanda form, a panel that always beautifies the central cell in all early Pallava temples, has been repeated over and over again by their sculptors. Almost preserved, though far from complete, amongst all the surviving fragments of painting of the Pallava period, there is one of a Somāskanda from the Kailāsanātha temple at Kāñchīpuram, typical of the other lithic Somāskandas we know from the temples of Rājasiṁha's time. The Somāskanda in the National Museum (Plate XIII) is the only stone carving of the kind and of this period found in any museum in the world outside the Pallava monuments where they abound.

Another similar sculpture of special importance (Plate XIV) illustrating the Pallava phase is a Bhikashāṭana who is engaging the attention of the wives of ṛishis who come out to offer him alms and wonder at his beauty.

A large seated Vishṇu is carved in relief in a manner that is characteristic of the later phase of Pallava art (Plate XV). It is a very pleasing figure of Vishṇu carrying his usual weapons in the manner he does in this phase of Pallava art.

The Gurjara-Pratīhāras who succeeded to a large empire left by the Vardhanas in the North, are known for their vast contribution to early medieval North Indian art, particularly in the Uttar Pradesh, Rājasthān, Punjāb and Gujarāt. A fine example of early medieval sculpture is a recently acquired Śiva as Rāvaṇānugrahamūrti (Plate XVI), composing the ten-headed monster, that shook the mighty Kailāsa in his pride, but finally stayed to sing the glory of the Lord, in *Sāma* hymns in musical notes, to win the pleasure and mercy of Śiva, and get a release from the pressure of the toe, which brought the weight of the mountain on him for his offence. The witnessing gods around have been characteristically portrayed in the idiom of an earlier phase, continuing great traditions kept alive by successive generations of craftsmen.

The bronze image of Vishṇu with consorts, though greatly worn, is still important as the only one belonging to the period which can be definitely dated in the time of Mahīpāladeva (Plate XVII). It is a recent acquisition in the National Museum.

From Rājasthān, a fine example of Gurjara-Pratihāra sculpture is a marriage of Śiva with Pārvatī, which is another new acquisition of great beauty in the National Museum (Plate XVIII).

A tenth century Chāhamāna sculpture of great aesthetic quality is a frieze from the ruins of the Śiva temple on the hill called Harsha in the neighbourhood of Sikar.It represents a group of warriors entertained by musicians, all the figures arranged in a rhythmic sway of bodily movement most charming to behold (Plate XIX).

Another similar addition to the collection in the National Museum is a Cheḍi sculpture in metal, representing Avalokiteśvara seated on a lotus(Plate XX). That he is young and *kūmārabhūta* is indicated by the side locks (*kākapaksha*) that he wears and the *vyāghranakha* or the tiger claws. It is extremely interesting that this bronze has the name of the sculptor, Droṇāditya, inscribed in clear letters of the 9th century.

An exquisite bronze almost of the period of transition from Pallava to Choḷa and nearer the earliest phase of Choḷa idiom is a Kāliya Kṛishṇa with a slender leg of the dancer balanced on the hoods of the snake on which the personified Nāgarāja is indicated (Plate XXI).

Very early Choḷa art is represented in the National Museum by two more important bronzes, Somāskanda (Plate XXII), and Naṭarāja (Plate XXIII). This Naṭarāja from Tiruvaraṅguḷam, dancing in the *chatura* pose, is unique and there is no other figure in metal in that dancing pose anywhere else. Aesthetically also it is a perfect example of graceful modelling, balance and movement. It is a symbolic representation of Śiva as the Creator, Protector and Destroyer, indicated by the drum, the hands in grace and carrying the flame, the pointing fingers assuring protection to those who seek salvation at his feet. Ignorance which dwarfs us is represented as a dwarf, annihilated under his foot, and this act coincides with the dawn of knowledge indicated by a crescent growing into a full moon or the fulness of wisdom. The concept of Naṭarāja became so popular in the South, particularly in the Choḷa period, that there is no temple anywhere that does not have a hall forNaṭarāja, the bronze representation of the dancing Lord.

The medieval art from the hilly area, in the neighbourhood of Kashmir, is illustrated by an exquisite bronze from Chambā representing a Devī as the female counterpart of Sadāśiva (Plate XXIV). It is inscribed and can be dated about 1000 A.D.

The Cheḍis who ruled from Bundelkhand had neighbours in Madhya Pradesh that enriched Mahobā and Khajurāho with magnificent monuments. These are the Chandrātreyas also known as Chandellas. A unique Chandella sculpture in the National Museum, recently acquired, represents Harihara seated in *ālīḍha*, a very rare form (Plate XXV). Harihara is not so unusal, but Harihara seated in *āliḍha* is certainly very rare. We know that the Tripurāntaka form of Śiva portrays the great Lord as the mightiest bowman, overcoming the loftiest of the titans, Tripurāsuras, an achievement for which Śiva is chiefly praised in poetic compositions by some of the most renowned poets in Sanskrit literature. If Śiva is known as the greatest bowman, wielding as he does a mountain as bow, Merudhanvā, Vishṇu equally wields a powerful weapon of horn as a great bowman and is called Śārṅgapāṇi. The warrior pose *ālīḍha* is most eloquent expression of the might of a bowman. In a combination of both these great bowmen, the *ālīḍha* pose chosen is most suggestive. In praising the bowman pose of the great prince Raghu, Kālīdāsa cannot refrain picturing him as Śiva Tripurāri in his warrior pose *ālīḍha atishṭhad ālīḍhaviśeshaśobhinā vapuhprakarsheṇa viḍambi-teśvarah.*

In Eastern India, the contemporary rulers were the Pālas, whose early phase of art is here represented by an Avalokiteśvara (Plate XXVI), whose calm and serene countenance and chiselled features at once proclaim the charm of early Pāla sculpture.

A fine example of a rare theme in medieval sculpture is a Pāla Gajalakshmī, bathed by celestial elephants and flanked by the personified treasures, Ṣankha and Padma (Plate XXVII).

Another early example of Pāla art is Vishṇu with his hands resting on personified *āyudhapurushas*, Chakra and Gadā. This still reveals earlier Gupta characteristics, like the wig-like hair, short crown and so forth (Plate XXVIII).

A bronze from Kurkihār of rare beauty representing Haragaurī (Plate XXIX), not long ago purchased for the National Museum, is typical of the best craftsmanship during the Pāla period.

One of the most lovely Gāhaḍavāla sculptures dug up at Sārnāth is Vajratārā, a typical example of deities in a complex Buddhist iconography that had developed (Plate XXX).

Another fine example is a Jaina Sarasvatī, delicately carved in marble and presenting the fineness of a jeweller's work (Plate XXXI).

Late medieval art of the 12th century of Rājasthān is represented by a feminine head of the Gāhaḍavāla school, a dainty one with a flower-decked braid (Plate XXXII).

The later phase of Western Chāḷukya sculpture in the South is represented in the National Museum by an exquisite door lintel, with very fine carving, from which a central panel of Śiva dancing is here chosen (Plate XXXIII). Devī watches as multiarmed Śiva dances. It is the grace of the goddess that she watches her Lord's dance like a mother. The mother out of her mercy refrains herself from partaking of whatever is injurious to the child and conversely takes in such as would benefit the child in the womb.

The Hoysaḷas, who were great builders of monuments, created temples profusely decorated but in the Chāḷukyan style, being successors of the Western Chālukyas in the Mysore area. The huntress from Haḷebid (Plate XXXIV) is a fine example of this school.

The Kākatīyas, who followed the traditions of the Western Chāḷukyas, having been feudatories under this power for a while had created magnificent temples in their realm, like those at Wārangal, Pālampet and other places. This distinctive school is represented in the National Museum by a magnificent lintel of the 13th century from Wārangal, a panel from which is chosen here (Plate XXXV).

In Eastern India, south of the Pāla empire, was the kingdom of the Eastern Gaṅgas whose imposing monuments, like those at Bhubanesvar, Puri and Koṇārak in Orissa are noteworthy. The art of the Eastern Gaṅgas is here represented by two magnificent carvings, one of Varuṇānī (Plate XXXVI), the consort of Varuṇa on her *Makara* vehicle and Narasiṁha, the great and powerful king, who built the temple of wonder at Koṇārak (Plate XXXVII). Narasiṁha was not only a gay prince, as observed in the scene of his life in the harem, enjoying a swing, but a great connoisseur of art and literature, a powerful warrior, devotee of great catholicity, at once devoted to several forms of the Supreme Being that his ancestors had worshipped, without any special prejudice to his own preference for the God of light, Sūrya, to whom he raised a mighty temple at Konārak.

This Sūrya is a fine carving with soft and delicate decorative details, typical of Orissan work (Plate XXXVIII).

Among the recent acquisitions in the National Museum, a unique bronze of the Vijayanagara period, the only one of its kind to represent the noble theme of Bharata as the ideal brother, carrying the wooden sandals of his brother Rāma, as the sovereign of the State, on whose behalf he was to rule, is here a typical example of the simple, but effective, somewhat, stylised work, of this late medieval period of Indian art (Plate XXXIX). As we know the Vijayanagara emperors represent the last great phase of Hindu hegemony in India. The affluence of this great period of art is easily visualised in the numerous monuments that stud practically the whole of South India and the Deccan. This bronze is a worthy example of Vijayanagara phase of Indian art.

The plates that accompany this album constitute a delightful bevy of chosen pictures to illustrate, through the best examples available in the National Museum, a comprehensive picture of the styles and schools of art, geographically and historically distributed all over the country in space as well as in time.

C. SIVARAMAMURTI

PLATE I

The division of the relics of Buddha, Śunga, 2nd century B.C., Bharhut, Madhya Pradesh.

PLATE II

Prince and Princess in harem with attendants, Sātavāhana, 2nd century B.C., Pitalkhora, Western India.

Terminal of Architrave, Sātavāhana. 2nd–1st century B.C., Sāñchī, Madhya Pradesh.

PLATE IV

Asita's visit, Sātavāhana, 2nd century A.D., Amarāvatī, Andhra Pradesh.

a. Srī Lakshmī, Kushāna, Ist century A.D., Mathurā, Uttar Pradesh.

b. Mother and Child, Kushāna, 2nd century A.D., Mathurā, Uttar Pradesh.

PLATE VI

Kubera, Lord of Wealth, Kushāna, 2nd century A.D., Mathurā, Uttar Pradesh.

Sundarī's toilet and Nanda's conversion, Gandhāra, 2nd century A.D.

PLATE VIII

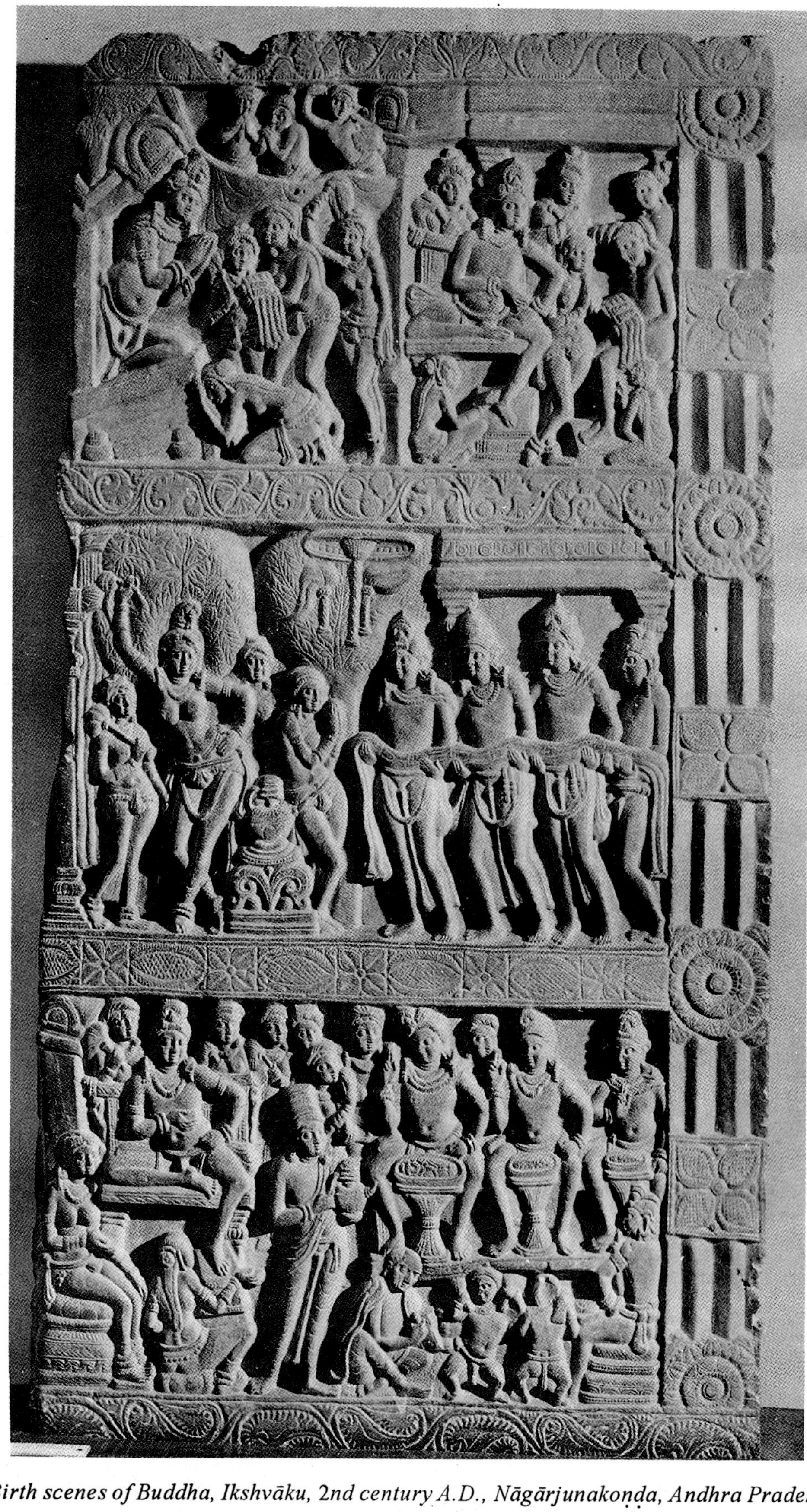

Birth scenes of Buddha, Ikshvāku, 2nd century A.D., Nāgārjunakoṇḍa, Andhra Pradesh.

Vishṇu, Gupta, 5th century A.D., Mathurā, Uttar Pradesh.

a. Avalokiteśvara, Gupta, 5th century A.D., Sārnāth, Uttar Pradesh.

b. Buddha, Vākāṭaka, 5th century A.D., Phopnar, Madhya Pradesh.

Mother and Child, Maitraka, 6th century A.D., Sāmalājī, Gujarat.

PLATE XII

Flying Vidyādharas, early Western Chaḷukya, 6th century A.D., Aihole, Mysore.

Somāskanda, Pallava, 7th century A.D., from near Kāñchīpuram, Tamil Nāḍu.

PLATE XIV

Bhikshāṭana, Pallava, 7th century A.D., from near Kāñchīpuram, Tamil Nāḍu.

Seated Vishṇu, Pallava, 8th century A.D., from near Kāñchīpuram, Tamil Nāḍu.

Rāvaṇānugrahamūrti, Gurjara-Pratīhāra, 10*th century A.D., Uttar Pradesh.*

Vishṇu with consorts, Gurjara-Pratīhāra, 10*th century A.D., Uttar Pradesh.*

Marriage of Śiva, Gurjara-Pratīhāra, 10*th century A.D., Rājasthān.*

Warriors and Musicians, Chāhamāna, 10*th century A.D., Sikar, Rājasthān.*

PLATE XX

Avalokītesvara, Cheḍī, 9th century A.D., Sirpur, Madhya Pradesh.

Kālīya Krishna, Chola, 10*th century A.D., Tamil Nādu.*

Somāskanda, Choḷa, 10*th century A.D., Tamil Nāḍu.*

Naṭarāja, Choḷa, 10*th century A.D., Tiruvarāṅgulam, Tamil Nāḍu.*

PLATE XXIV

Devī, Utpala, 1000 A.D., Chambā, Himachal Pradesh.

Harihara, Chandella, 10*th*-11*th century A.D., Madhya Pradesh.*

PLATE XXVI

Avalokiteśvara, Pāla, 8th century A.D., Nālandā, Bihar.

Gajālakshmī, Pāla, 9th century A.D., Bihar.

PLATE XXVIII

Vishṇu with āyudhapurushas, Pāla, 9th century A.D., Bihar.

Haragaurī, Pāla, 10th century A.D., Kurkihār, Bihar

PLATE XXX

Vajratārā, Gāhaḍavāla, 12th century A.D., Sārnāth, Uttar Pradesh.

Sarasvatī, Gāhadavāla, 12*th century A.D., Bikaner, Rājasthān.*

Flower bedecked Braid, Gāhaḍavāla, 12th century A.D., Bikaner, Rājasthān.

Siva Dancing, Western Chāḷukya, 12th century A.D., Hampī, Mysore.

The Huntress, Hoysaḷa, 12th century A.D., Haḷebīḍ, Mysore.

Śiva Dancing, Kākatīya, 13*th century A.D., Wārangal, Andhra Pradesh.*

Varuṇānī, Eastern Gaṅga, 13th century A.D., Koṇārak, Orissa.

Narasiṁha on Swing in harem, Eastern Gaṅga, 13*th century A.D., Koṇārak, Orissa.*

Sūrya, Eastern Gaṅga, 13th century A.D., Koṇārak, Orissa.

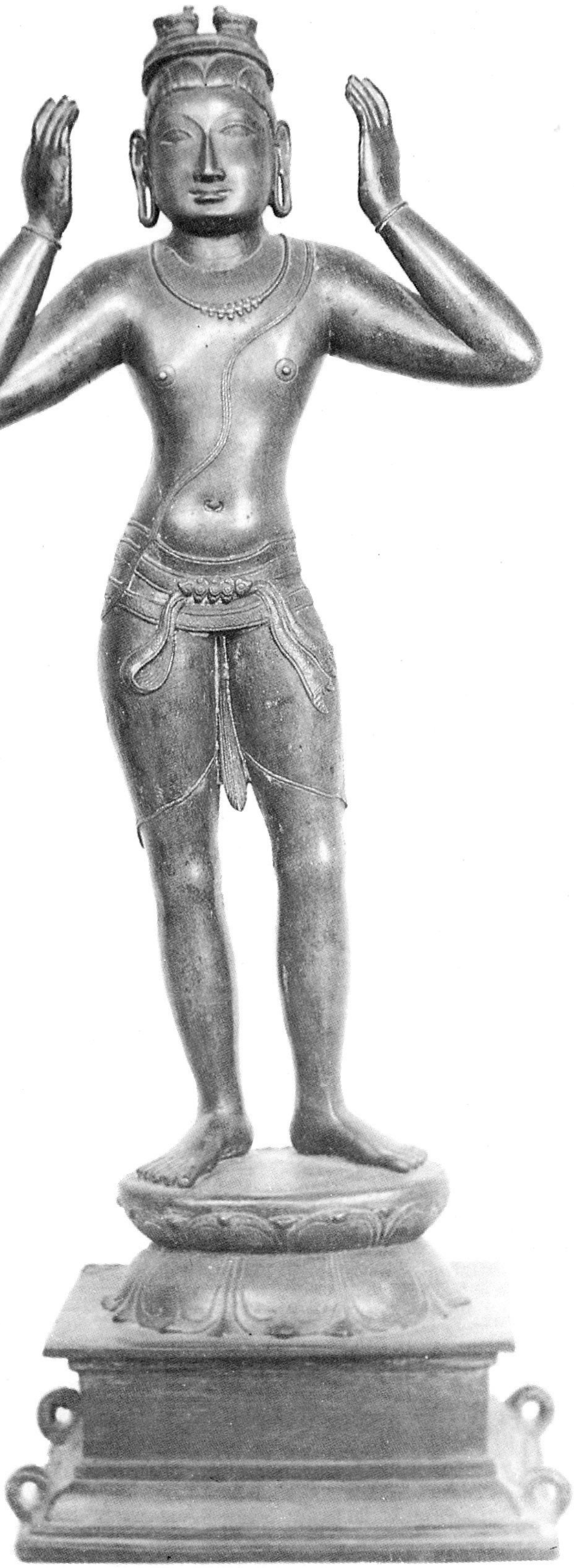

Bharata, Vijayanagara, 14*th century A.D., Tamil Nāḍu.*

NOTES ON PLATES

I. *The Division of the relics of Buddha, Śuṅga, 2nd century B.C., Bharhut, Madhya Pradesh.*

The carving of this coping piece is typical of the richest phase of early sculpture in the 2nd century B.C. The reliquaries carried on elephants caparisoned and the dancing and music for the funeral of Buddha reveal the inordinate reverence for the Master and the deep impress of his teaching and his magnetism in the eagerness for securing the relics of the Master.

II. *Prince and Princess in harem with attendants, Sātavāhana, 2nd century B.C., Pitalkhora, Western India.*

It is a fine example of early Sātavāhana work giving a peep into the life of the age. The couch with rich coverlet and the typical jewellery mentioned in the *Arthaśāstra* shown here is very interesting.

III. *Terminal of Architrave, Sātavāhana, 2nd—Ist century B.C., Sāñchī, Madya Pradesh.*

The *toraṇa* of the Sāñchī gateway provides a vivid picture of the life in the Sātavāhana period. The fact that this has been carved by ivory carvers of Vidiśā as given in the inscription, enables us to judge the delicacy of carving in softer material repeated here in stone.

IV. *Asita's visit, Sātsavāhana, 2nd century A.D., Amarāvatī, Andhra Pradesh.*

This is a typical well-carved upright from the famous rail of the Amarāvatī *stūpa*. It illustrates, an important incident from Buddha's life, sage Asita's visit to see the baby Siddhrtha, who was later to become the Enlightened One. This is a fine example to illustrate the delicacy of Sātavāhana art in the Kṛishṇā valley in about the second century A.D.

Va. *Śrī Lakshmī, Kushāna, Ist century A.D., Mathurā, Uttar Pradesh.*

This is among the most important early representations of Lakshmī and is also very suggestive. This *pūrṇaghaṭa* or the brimming vessel suggesting plenty and prosperity indicates also the river goddess as a mother goddess. Maternity is eulogized deeply by a pun on the word *payas* meaning both milk and water. The peacock shown as a motif on the armlet of the goddess as well as on the back of the scuplture itself suggests again joy and prosperity as also the smile on her face.

Vb. *Mother and Child, Kushāna, 2nd century A.D., Mathurā, Uttar Pradesh.*

This popular theme of mother and child has been very delicately handled and the eagerness of the child to receive a plaything as almost reflected in the joy of the mother and her companion watching the child scrambling for the toy with a rare satisfaction.

VI. *Kubera, Lord of Wealth, Kushāna, 2nd century A.D., Mathurā, Uttar Pradesh.*

The rotund belly, the wigged hair, the half-closed eyes are exceedingly well depicted by the sculptor who has a dig at the opulent. Kubera means one of ugly form and a short fat dwarf cannot be rated charming.

VII. *Sundarī's toilet and Nanda's conversion, Gandhāra, 2nd century A.D.*

Note the attitude of the *Prasādhikās* (decorators) attending on Sundarī and the worshipful attitude of Nanda whom Buddha converted against his will.

VIII. *Birth scenes of Buddha, Ikshvāku, 2nd century A.D., Nāgārjunakoṇḍa, Andhra Pradesh.*

This is one of the finest sculptures representing Ikshvāku art which closely follows the style of the Amarāvatī sculptor. This coping piece divided into panels narrates the scenes belonging to the birth of Buddha in a very interesting manner. The sculptor as a narrator excelled like the poet or the chronicler. The symbolic representation of Buddha by the feet and the significance of 'umbrella and *chaurī*' should be specially noted.

IX. *Vishṇu, Gupta, 5th century A.D., Mathurā, Uttar Pradesh.*

This is undoubtedly the most magnificent of individual sculptures of the Gupta period representing Vishṇu. The typical crown, the *vanamālā,* the charming strings of pearls twirled round the neck, the long and elegant *yajñopavīta* are all characteristic of early Gupta work.

Xa. *Avalokiteśvara, Gupta, 5th century A.D., Sārnāth, Uttar Pradesh.*

There is rarely any sculpture of the Gupta period to beat this in grace, charm, pose and feeling. The locks of hair settling on the shoulder, the golden chain as *yajñopavīta,* the soft modelling of the limbs, the serene face are all characteristic of early Gupta art.

Xb. *Buddha, Vākāṭaka, 5th century A.D., Phopnar, Madhya Pradesh.*

This is one of the very few examples of Vākāṭaka sculpture in metal yet dicovered. In feeling and workmanship the bronze recalls similar figures from

Ajaṇṭā and Ellorā caves of the same period. The cherubs fluttering above the umbrella add to the charm of this unique bronze.

XI. *Mother and Child, Maitraka, 6th century A.D., Sāmalājī, Gujarat.*

Some of the finest examples of Indian art have been obtained in Roḍā and Sāmalājī, and this mother and child with beaming face glorify motherhood, the grace of a child, and the joy of the age of innocence. The sweet fragrant leaves adorning the braid of the mother suggest also the fragrance of the theme.

XII. *Flying Vidyādharas, early Western Chāḷukya, 6th century A.D., Aihoḷe, Mysore.*

This group from a temple ceiling is unbeaten for the grace of the sculptor's art. The lines composing the flying figures, the clouds and the fluttering garments have been well handled by the sculptor to suggest movement.

XIII. *Somāskanda, Pallava, 7th century A.D., from near Kāñchīpuram, Tamil Nāḍu.*

The theme of Śiva with Umā and Skanda was very popular in the Pallava period and it is repeated in all the central cells of shrines. In these early representations of Somāskanda, Vishṇu and Brahmā are shown in the background in the sculptor's anxiety to represent the Trinity together everywhere. It is a theme of the unstinting affection of parents completely bestowed on the child which increases manifold and radiates towards them.

XIV. *Bhikshāṭana, Pallava, 7th century A.D., from near Kāñchīpuram, Tamil Nāḍu.*

The Bhikshāṭana theme was again a very popular one in South Indian sculpture and this is one of the earliest representations. In later Choḷa sculpture there are equally beautiful representations of Bhikshāṭana, sometimes with a number of ṛishipatnis or wives of ṛishis crowding around him. This is very simple and effective.

XV. *Seated Vishṇu, Pallava, 8th century A.D., from near Kāñchīpuram, Tamil Nāḍu.*

Towards the end of the Pallava period similar figures appear in profusion. Of these the seated figure from Satyamaṅgalam now in the Madras Museum is an excellent example.

XVI. *Rāvaṇānugrahamūrti, Gurjara-Pratīhāra, 10th century A.D., Uttar Pradesh.*

This is a fine example illustrating the art of one of the greatest medieval schools. The grouping of deities above recalls early Gupta and Vākāṭaka traditions. The theme is a very popular one and examples occur in almost every school. A sculpture from Kailāśa at Ellorā is very famous.

XVII. *Vishṇu with consorts, Gurjara-Pratīhāra, 10th century A.D., Uttar Pradesh.*

Though the figures are worn, it is very important on account of the inscription which gives the name of Mahīpāladeva in whose time the brozne was fashioned. It is, thus, very helpful in the study of bronzes for dating them on the strength of inscriptions and corresponding styles.

XVIII. *Marriage of Śiva, Gurjara-Pratīhāra, 10th century A.D., Rājasthān.*

As in the case of Rāvaṇānugrahamūrti, here is a delightful arrangement of gods witnessing the impressive ceremony from above the clouds. It recalls similar earlier mode and suggests the continuity of tradition.

XIX. *Warriors and musicians. Chāhamāna, 10th century A.D., Sikar, Rājasthān.*

A fine example of grouping of figures in action in a long frieze.

XX. *Avalokīteśvara, Chedī, 9th century A.D., Sirpur, Madhya Pradesh.*

This is an excellent example of metal work in the Cheḍī kingdom with the name of the sculptor Dronāditya inscribed on it.

XXI. *Kālīya Kṛishṇa, Choḷa, 10th century A.D., Tamil Nāḍu.*

The delicate treatment of the figure and the charm of the Nāgarāja represented against the snake hoods are noteworthy.

XXII. *Somāskanda, Choḷa, 10th century A.D., Tamil Nāḍu.*

This is a typical example of dedicated work in the early phase of Choḷa art. Metal images of Somāskanda were very popular in the Choḷa period.

XXIII. *Naṭarāja, Choḷa, 10th century A.D., Tiruvarañguḷam, Tamil Nāḍu.*

This is a unique image as there is no other in metal to represent Naṭarāja in the *chatura* pose of dancing. This ranks among the most important Naṭarāja images in the world and is a very fine example of the earlier phase of Choḷa art.

XXIV *Devī, Utpala, 1000 A.D., Chambā., Himachal Pradesh.*

This is a fine example of the medieval art of

the Himālayan region near about Chambā and Kashmir. Inscriptions in Śāradā characters of about 1000 A.D. add to the interest of this bronze.

XXV. *Harihara, Chandella, 10th-11th century A.D., Madhya Pradesh.*

This is a very fine example of the delicate work of the Chandella sculptor who has created the great monuments of Khajurāho and Mahobā. The combination of Śiva and Vishṇu with stress on the prowess of both in bowmanship is delightfully meaningful.

XXVI. *Avalokīteśvara, Pāla, 8th century A.D., Nālandā, Bihar.*

This is probably the best representation of Kumārabhūta Avalokiteśvara with suggestive sidelocks representing all that is charming in early Pāla sculpture from this great centre of sculptural work.

XXVII. *Gajālakshmī, Pāla, 9th century A.D., Bihar.*

A fine example of a rare theme in medieval northern sculpture, with all the early features clearly portrayed, as well as the *nidhis* Śaṅkha and Padma flanking her, while the celestial elephants empty pitchers of water over her head, the lotus symbolising water on her braid.

XXVIII. *Vishṇu with āyudhapurushas, Pāla, 9th century A.D., Bihar.*

A typical example of early workmanship with short crown, curls of hair wig-like resting on shoulders, prominent *vanamālā*, hands resting on personified Sudarśana (wheel) and Kaumodakī (club).

XXIX. *Haragaurī, Pāla, 10th century A.D., Kurkihār, Bihar.*

Though a miniature it is in the best traditions of Pāla work beautifully illustrated in the large collection of Kurkihār bronzes in the Patna Museum.

XXX. *Vajratārā, Gāhaḍavāla, 12th century A.D., Sārnāth, Uttar Pradesh.*

This is a fine sculpture illustrating a Buddhist deity in a spirited way, with the element of decoration more advanced than in earlier sculpture, but nevertheless pleasing.

XXXI. *Sarasvatī, Gāhadavāla, 12th century A.D., Bikaner, Rājasthān.*

It is a carving executed exceedingly well to represent Vāgdevī of the Jain pantheon. This is a very delicate work in marble.

XXXII. *Flower bedecked Braid, Gāhaḍavāla, 12th century A.D., Bikaner, Rājasthān.*

It is a rare representation of the beauty of feminine braid adorned with a variety of flowers and pearls. This pleasing theme has been very well executed by the sculpture.

XXXIII. *Śiva Dancing, Western Chāḷukya, 12th century A.D., Hampī, Mysore.*

This is the central part of a large exquisitely carved lintel of temple doorway from a Western Chāḷukya temple. It is typical of the pleasing decorative work of the later Chāḷukyas of which the best known is from Kuruvaṭṭi.

XXXIV. *The Huntress, Hoysaḷa, 12th century A.D., Haḷebīḍ, Mysore.*

Note the quaint dress composed of leaves that the forest folk wear. The figure, a charming damsel decked in jewels to enhance her natural feminine grace, is in typical decorative style characteristic of Hoysala art. A huntress, she examines her bows and arrows.

XXXV. *Śiva Dancing, Kākatīya, 13th century A.D., Wārangal, Andha Pradesh.*

This central part of a large lintel showing the Trinity dancing is typical of the Kākatīya workmanship as seen in temples at Pālampeṭ, Hanaṃkoṇḍā and other places.

XXXVI. *Varuṇānī, Eastern Gaṅga, 13th century A.D., Koṇārak, Orissa.*

It is of rare iconographic interest and aesthetically also is of a very high order.

XXXVII. *Narasiṁha on Swing in harem, Eastern Gaṅga, 13th century A.D., Koṇārak, Orissa.*

Narasiṁha, the great builder of the Koṇārak Temple, was one of the most outstanding monarchs of this dynasty, and among the several panels illustrating his life that decorate the temple at Koṇārak this is noteworthy. This illustrates the capacity of the Eastern Gaṅga sculptor to create portraits giving a peep into the characteristic traits of the individual to reveal his personality.

XXXVIII. *Sūrya, Eastern Gaṅga, 13th century A.D., Koṇārak, Orissa.*

This is one of the finest carvings from Koṇārak, being the deity intended for the sanctum. The decorative details being soft and delicate do not detract from its aesthetic value. The attendants, Daṇḍa, Piṅgala and the queens Chhāyā and Suvarchasā as well as the charioteer Aruṇa managing the seven horses make up a delightful group.

XXXIX. *Bharata, Vijayanagara, 14th century A.D., Tamil Nādu.*

This is a unique bronze in the best traditions of early Vijayanagara art. It is a rare theme represented with great delicacy and feeling. Rāma himself has paid the highest tribute to Bharata as a brother and this bronze fully radiates the affection and reverence of the younger brother to the elder.

Colour Plates

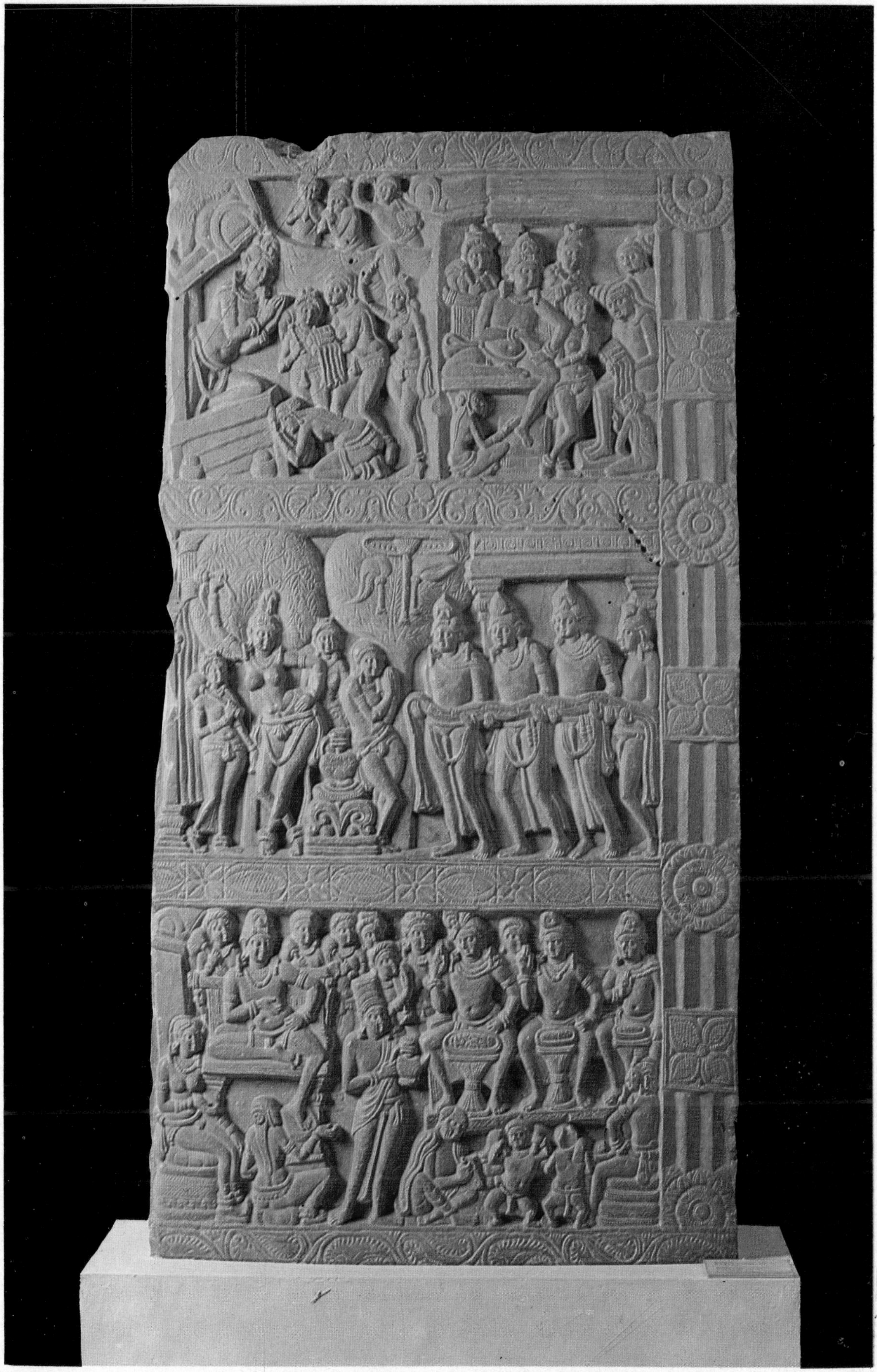

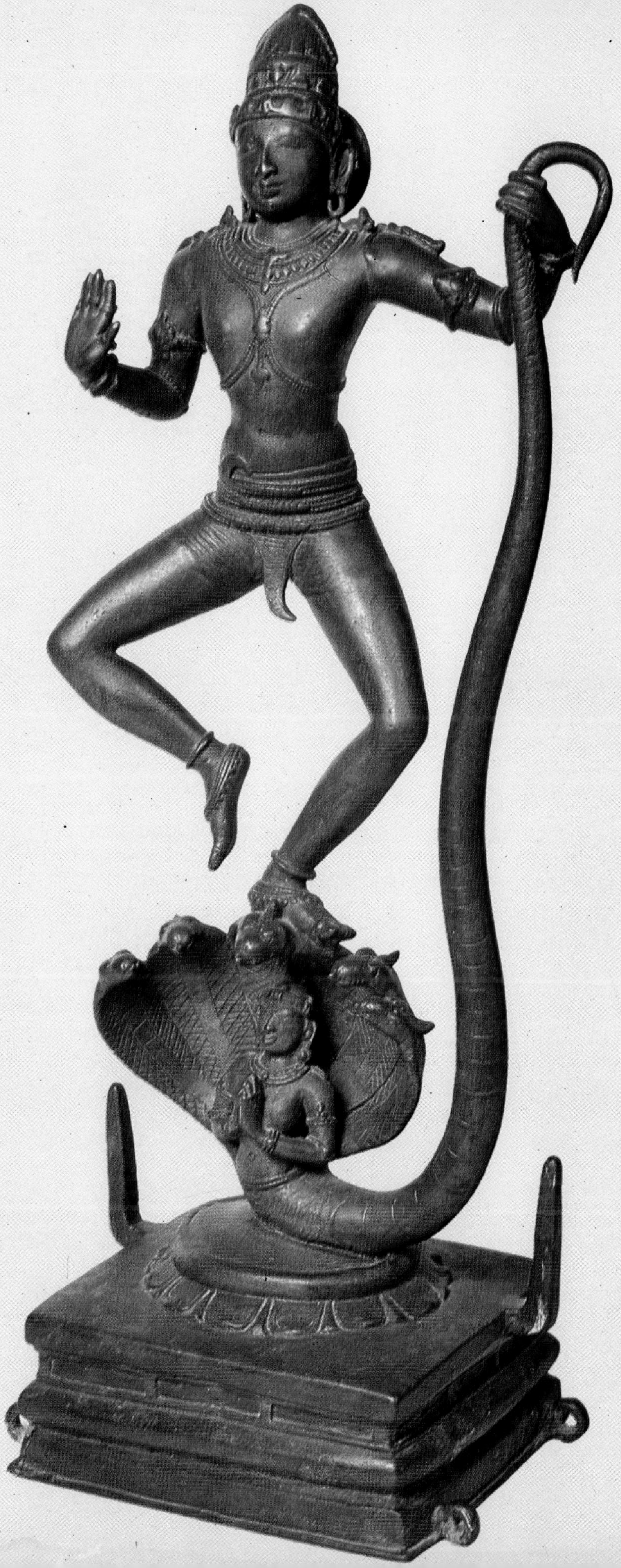